WeightWatchers®

fast & fabulous

60 delicious meals in 30 minutes or less

D1303049

SIMON & SCHUSTER
A CBS COMPANY

Tamsin Burnett-Hall

Introduction

Fast & Fabulous is a fantastic new cookbook with 60 recipes that can be prepared in 30 minutes or less. It's the perfect cookbook for when you are looking for a healthy and delicious meal but don't have lots of time.

An ideal, everyday kitchen companion. Each recipe clearly indicates the time it takes to prepare and the 'flipable' pages make it easy to decide what to cook depending on how much time you have. With its convenient format, you can stand it next to your cooker, making it easier to follow the recipes. There is no need to worry about anything splashing on it, with the wipe clean pages this versatile cookbook will look good as new.

Fast & Fabulous is perfect whether you are following the *POINTS*® **Plan** or the **Core Plan**™. There are 60 recipes to choose from, including over 25 vegetarian recipes, all with a clear *POINTS* value. And over 25 are suitable for the **Core Plan** with the distinctive Core tick by the title. You can choose from tasty lunches and light bites, satisfying main meals or scrumptious dessert and still lose weight.

lunches and light bites

Transform your lunchtimes with these appetizing recipes including Cajun steak muffin, Roasted pepper couscous salad, or Chinese chicken noodle soup. They're ideal if you are looking for something light. There's lots to choose from and all are quick and easy to prepare in under 15 minutes.

Scrumptious lunches and light bites. Index by **POINTS** values.

Serves 1

Takes 4 minutes

142 calories per serving

2 **POINTS** values per serving

2 **POINTS** values per recipe

1 x 80 g can tuna in spring
    water or brine

$^1/_2$ celery stick

$^1/_2$ eating apple

1 teaspoon grain mustard

2 tablespoons very low fat
    plain fromage frais

salt and freshly ground
    black pepper

Tuna crunch filling

This versatile filling, which makes a small can of tuna go a long way, is based on the famous New York Waldorf salad.

1. Drain the tuna, chop the celery and core and dice the apple.
2. Mix the mustard into the fromage frais then stir in the flaked tuna, celery, apple, and season to taste.

serving suggestion *spoon on to a medium size (225 g/8 oz) jacket potato for an extra* **POINTS** *value of 2$^1/_2$.*

takes only
4
minutes

Serves 1

Takes 5 minutes

115 calories per serving

2 **POINTS** values per serving

2 **POINTS** values per recipe

Ⓨ vegan

low fat cooking spray

$^1/_2$ red pepper *deseeded and diced*

3 spring onions *sliced*

$^1/_2$ teaspoon Cajun spice mix

1 x 200 g can reduced sugar and salt baked beans

Tex Mex beans

Spice up a can of beans for a speedy lunch and serve on a medium (225 g/8 oz) jacket potato for an extra **POINTS** value of $2^1/_2$, or over a medium portion (150 g/$5^1/_2$ oz) of cooked brown rice, for an extra **POINTS** value of 3.

❶ Lightly coat a small saucepan with low fat cooking spray and stir fry the pepper and spring onions for 2 minutes.

❷ Stir the Cajun spice into the vegetables, tip in the baked beans and heat through for 1–2 minutes, then serve immediately.

tip *If you don't have any Cajun spice mix, you can use $^1/_2$ teaspoon of cumin seeds or ground cumin, plus a pinch of chilli powder, in its place.*

takes only **5** minutes

Serves 1

Takes 5 minutes

362 calories per serving

6 **POINTS** values per serving

6 **POINTS** values per recipe

Ⓨ vegan

$^1/_2$ x 410 g can mixed pulses

$^1/_2$ x 198 g can sweetcorn
   with peppers

75 g (2$^3/_4$ oz) cherry tomatoes

$^1/_2$ medium ripe avocado

2 tablespoons fat free French
   dressing

1 Little Gem lettuce heart
   leaves separated

Fiesta bean salad

This salad is a colourful blend of salad vegetables and storecupboard ingredients.

1 Rinse and drain the pulses, drain the sweetcorn, halve the cherry tomatoes and dice the avocado.

2 Mix the pulses, sweetcorn, cherry tomatoes and avocado together with 1 tablespoon of the dressing.

3 Place the lettuce leaves in a bowl, drizzle with the second tablespoon of dressing then pile the pulse mixture on top to serve.

takes only
5
minutes

15 g (¹/₂ oz) mature half fat
   cheese *grated finely*
40 g (1¹/₂ oz) wafer thin
   smoked ham
1 tomato *sliced*
handful wild rocket leaves
   (about 10 g)
1 medium soft flour tortilla
salt and freshly ground
   black pepper

Ham & cheese tostadas

A tostada is a Mexican version of a toasted sandwich, using a soft flour tortilla in place of bread. Filled with melting cheese and ham, this is ideal served with a zero **POINTS** value mixed salad.

1 Preheat a non stick frying pan on the hob. Arrange the cheese, ham, tomato and rocket over half the tortilla, season, and fold over to make a half moon shape.

2 Add to the hot pan and press down well, then dry fry for 1 minute on both sides. Cut into wedges to serve.

Ⓥ **variation** *For a vegetarian version, replace the wafer thin ham with 1 heaped tablespoon of canned beans, such as kidney or black-eyed beans. The* **POINTS** *value will remain the same.*

Serves 1

Takes 6 minutes

247 calories per serving

4¹/₂ **POINTS** values per serving

4¹/₂ **POINTS** values per recipe

¹/₄–¹/₂ teaspoon Cajun spice
   mix

1 x 60 g (2 oz) sandwich
   steak or minute steak
   trimmed

low fat cooking spray

1 English muffin *white or*
   wholemeal split

1 tablespoon 0% fat Greek
   yogurt

1 tomato *sliced*

1 leaf from a round lettuce
   or shredded Iceberg
   lettuce

Cajun steak muffin

A great treat for a speedy lunch, especially at the weekend.

❶ Sprinkle the Cajun spice mix (use ¹/₄ or ¹/₂ teaspoon, depending on desired degree of spiciness) over both sides of the steak.

❷ Preheat a non stick frying pan and lightly coat with low fat cooking spray. Fry the steak for 1–1¹/₂ minutes each side, to your liking.

❸ Meanwhile, lightly toast the muffin then spread the yogurt on to the cut sides. Top with the sliced tomato, lettuce and steak, and eat straightaway.

Ⓨ **variation** *For a vegetarian version, replace the steak with a large flat mushroom, sliced and fried as above. This will be a **POINTS** value of 2¹/₂ per serving.*

takes only
6
minutes

Serves 1

Takes 6 minutes

268 calories per serving

4 *POINTS* values per serving

4 *POINTS* values per recipe

40 g (1¹/₂ oz) fine egg
  noodles *broken roughly*

60 g (2 oz) baby corn *sliced
  thinly*

¹/₂ chicken stock cube *made
  up to 300 ml (10 fl oz) with
  boiling water*

1 teaspoon soy sauce

75 g (2³/₄ oz) cooked
  chicken breast *sliced*

2 spring onions *sliced*

Chinese chicken noodle soup

This Chinese style favourite makes for a quick and very filling lunch or light supper.

1 Add the noodles and baby corn to a pan of boiling water and cook for 3 minutes. Drain and rinse in cold water.

2 Pour the stock into the saucepan, add the soy sauce and bring to a simmer. Mix in the chicken, spring onion, cooked noodles and baby corn and heat through for 1–2 minutes until piping hot. Pour into a bowl and serve.

Ⓨ **variation** *For a vegetarian version, replace the cooked chicken with the same weight of sliced button mushrooms and use vegetable stock in place of the chicken stock. This will be a **POINTS** value of 2 per serving.*

takes only 6 minutes

Serves 1

Takes 6 minutes

183 calories per serving

3 **POINTS** values per serving

3 **POINTS** values per recipe

2 beef tomatoes

125 g (4$^{1}/_{2}$ oz) cooked peeled
   prawns

50 g (1$^{3}/_{4}$ oz) cucumber *diced*

$^{1}/_{2}$ lemon *grated zest and
   juice*

2 tablespoons low fat plain
   yogurt

pinch cayenne pepper

salt and freshly ground
   black pepper

Prawn stuffed tomatoes

Serve these summery stuffed tomatoes with four extra thin rye or wholemeal crispbreads for an additional **POINTS** value of 1.

1 Cut a lid off each tomato, then scoop out the seedy insides, using a teaspoon, and discard.

2 Toss the prawns together with the cucumber, lemon zest and juice, yogurt, cayenne and seasoning to taste then spoon this mixture inside the tomatoes to serve.

takes only
6
minutes

Serves 1

Takes 7 minutes

325 calories per serving

4 **POINTS** values per serving

4 **POINTS** values per recipe

50 g (1³/₄ oz) mini pasta
shapes, e.g. conchigliette

1 x 80 g can tuna in spring
water or brine *drained and
flaked*

for the dressing

¹/₂ teaspoon medium curry
powder

salt and freshly ground
black pepper

60 g (2 oz) low fat plain yogurt

¹/₂ red or yellow pepper
deseeded and diced

75 g (2³/₄ oz) cucumber *diced*

Curried tuna pasta salad

Quick and easy to prepare, this is a great pasta salad to take to work.

1 Add the pasta to a pan of boiling water and cook for 4–5 minutes until tender.

2 Meanwhile, make the dressing: mix the curry powder and seasoning into the yogurt, then stir in the diced pepper and cucumber.

3 Drain the pasta into a sieve and rinse in cold water. Shake dry then stir into the dressing, followed by the flaked tuna.

takes only
7
minutes

Serves 1

Takes 8 minutes

285 calories per serving

4$^1/_2$ **POINTS** values per serving

4$^1/_2$ **POINTS** values per recipe

50 g (1$^3/_4$ oz) couscous

60 g (2 oz) broccoli *cut into
small florets*

1 roasted red pepper in
brine, from a jar *drained
and sliced*

8 cherry tomatoes *halved*

1 tablespoon fresh basil
shredded

25 g (1 oz) feta cheese
crumbled

salt and freshly ground
black pepper

Roasted pepper couscous
salad

Perfect for a packed lunch, this flavoursome and colourful couscous salad makes a great change from everyday sandwiches.

1 Place the couscous in a bowl and pour in 75 ml (3 fl oz) boiling water. Stir, cover with a plate and leave to stand for 5 minutes to absorb the liquid and soften. Fluff up with a fork when ready.

2 Meanwhile, boil the broccoli in water for 3 minutes, drain and rinse in cold water. Mix into the couscous, followed by the roasted pepper, tomatoes, basil and feta cheese. Season and tip into a lidded plastic box. Chill until ready to serve.

tip *For a no-cook salad, replace the broccoli with diced raw courgette, cucumber or radishes. The **POINTS** value will remain the same.*

Serves 1

Takes 8 minutes

310 calories per serving

6 *POINTS* values per serving

6 *POINTS* values per recipe

$^1/_2$ lime *grated zest and juice*

2 tablespoons low fat plain
   yogurt

salt and freshly ground
   black pepper

$^1/_2$ ripe medium avocado
   sliced

4 Romaine lettuce leaves
   rinsed and shredded

75 g (2$^3/_4$ oz) cherry
   tomatoes *quartered*

100 g (3$^1/_2$ oz) cooked
   chicken breast *sliced*

Tangy chicken & avocado
salad

The lime and yogurt dressing gives this salad a really refreshing flavour.

1 Mix the lime zest and half the juice with the yogurt and seasoning to make a tangy dressing.

2 Toss the sliced avocado with the remaining lime juice.

3 Make a bed of shredded lettuce in a bowl then add the cherry tomatoes, avocado and sliced chicken. Drizzle on the dressing just before serving.

Pesto & roasted pepper bagel

Serves 1

Takes 12 minutes

300 calories per serving

4¹/₂ **POINTS** values per serving

4¹/₂ **POINTS** values per recipe

¹/₂ red pepper *deseeded*

1 medium bagel (80 g)

1 teaspoon pesto

25 g (1 oz) low fat soft cheese

15 g (¹/₂ oz) watercress

Roasted or grilled peppers have a lovely sweet flavour, and soften in the cooking process, which also makes them easier to digest.

1 Preheat the grill to its highest setting. Press the pepper half flat with your hand and place on the grill rack, skin side up, close to the heat.

2 Grill for about 5 minutes until the skin blackens and blisters. Remove from the heat, place in a bowl, cover and leave to cool for a few minutes. Peel off the skin then cut the pepper into strips.

3 Cut the bagel in half and toast lightly. Mix the pesto into the soft cheese then spread on the bottom half of the bagel. Add the red pepper strips and watercress to the bottom half of the bagel, cover with the top half and serve.

tip *If you don't have time to grill the pepper, you can buy jars of ready-roasted and peeled peppers in brine. These can also be added to salads, pasta sauces and stir-fries.*

takes only **12** minutes

Lemon chicken salad wrap

Serves 1

Takes 12 minutes

259 calories per serving

4½ **POINTS** values per serving

4½ **POINTS** values per recipe

salt and freshly ground
    black pepper
100 g (3½ oz) chicken mini
    fillets or chicken breast
    cut into strips
low fat cooking spray
½ lemon, grated zest + 1
    teaspoon juice
1 tablespoon low fat
    mayonnaise
1 medium soft flour tortilla
15 g (½ oz) young leaf
    spinach
25 g (1 oz) cucumber *cut into
    matchsticks*

Tortillas make a great alternative to sandwiches at lunchtime. Extra tortillas can be individually wrapped in cling film and frozen.

1 Preheat the grill to a high setting.

2 Lightly season the chicken, mist with low fat cooking spray and cook under the grill for 8–10 minutes, turning once, until cooked through. Cut the chicken into chunky pieces

3 Meanwhile, mix the lemon zest, juice and seasoning with the mayonnaise. Warm the tortilla to soften it, either by heating for 10–15 seconds either side in a hot dry frying pan, or by microwaving for 10 seconds.

4 Spread the lemon mayo over the tortilla then scatter the spinach, cucumber and chicken on top. Roll up and cut in half to serve.

tip *You can use 75 g (2¾ oz) cold, cooked chicken breast, sliced, in these wraps for a **POINTS** value of 5.*

takes only
12
minutes

1 wholemeal pitta

1 medium hard-boiled egg
   peeled

2 tablespoons very low fat
   plain fromage frais

1/4 teaspoon medium curry
   powder

salt and freshly ground
   black pepper

2 tablespoons hot mustard
   cress *snipped*

2 Little Gem lettuce leaves

Curried egg & cress pitta

For the perfect hard boiled egg, place in a small pan of cold water, bring to the boil and simmer for 6–7 minutes. Cool under cold running water to prevent a dark ring from forming around the yolk.

1 Lightly toast the pitta.

2 Meanwhile, mash the hard-boiled egg together with the fromage frais, curry powder and seasoning, using a fork. Stir in the cress.

3 Split the pitta bread open and tuck a lettuce leaves inside the pocket. Spoon in the curried egg and cress filling and serve.

takes only
12
minutes

Serves 4

Takes 15 minutes

165 calories per serving

2 **POINTS** values per serving

8 **POINTS** values per recipe

1 onion *chopped finely*

low fat cooking spray

850 ml (1¹/₂ pints) hot
   vegetable stock

1 x 400 g can chopped
   tomatoes

200 g (7 oz) frozen mixed
   vegetables (e.g. peas,
   sweetcorn, carrots
   and green beans)

1 x 410 g can flageolet or
   borlotti beans *drained and
   rinsed*

salt and freshly ground
   black pepper

2 tablespoons pesto sauce

Italian bean & vegetable soup

A chunky, hearty soup with a rustic touch, this will keep you feeling full for longer.

❶ In a large saucepan, fry the onion in low fat cooking spray over a high heat for 2–3 minutes. Add 4 tablespoons of the stock, cover the pan and cook for 3 minutes until softened.

❷ Mix in the tomatoes, vegetables, beans and remaining stock. Season, cover and simmer for 5 minutes or until the vegetables are tender.

❸ Ladle into bowls and top each bowlful with ¹/₂ tablespoon of pesto sauce to stir in as you eat.

takes only
15
minutes

Serves 2

Takes 15 minutes

260 calories per serving

4 **POINTS** values per serving

7^1/$_2$ **POINTS** values per recipe

60 g (2 oz) thin rice noodles

2 medium eggs, plus 2
  medium egg whites

salt and freshly ground
  black pepper

4 spring onions *chopped*

juice ^{1}/$_2$ lime

3 tablespoons coriander
  chopped

1 x 170 g can white meat
  crab in brine *drained*

low fat cooking spray

Crab egg rolls

These Vietnamese style lunch rolls are served at room temperature. They can be wrapped up and packed into a lunchbox if you wish.

1 Pour boiling water over the noodles to cover and leave to stand for 5 minutes until softened. Meanwhile, beat the eggs and egg whites with a little seasoning then stir in the spring onions. Drain the noodles, rinse in cold water and mix with the lime juice, coriander and crab meat. Season the mixture with freshly ground black pepper.

2 Spray a small non stick frying pan with low fat cooking spray. Pour in a quarter of the egg mixture, swirl around the pan and cook over a medium to high heat for 1 minute on the first side. Flip over and cook for a further 30 seconds. As each egg wrap is cooked, add a quarter of the crab noodle mixture and roll up, then repeat to make a total of four rolls.

takes only **15** minutes

Serves 2

Takes 10 minutes to prepare +
marinating, 8–10 minutes to cook

204 calories per serving

3 **POINTS** values per serving

5¹/₂ **POINTS** values per recipe

juice of 1 small lemon

1 teaspoon medium curry
    powder

¹/₄ teaspoon dried mint

salt and freshly ground
    black pepper

250 g (9 oz) rump steak
    trimmed and cut into 2.5cm
    (1 inch) cubes

1 red onion chopped roughly

1 red pepper deseeded and
    chopped roughly

Spiced beef kebabs

Serve these mildly spiced beef kebabs on a bed of crisp zero **POINTS** value mixed salad, accompanied by 1 tablespoon of low fat natural yogurt for an extra **POINTS** value of ¹/₂.

1 Preheat the grill to its highest setting.

2 Mix the lemon juice, curry powder, mint and seasoning together in a bowl. Stir in the diced steak, red onion and pepper and mix well to coat in the spice mixture.

3 Thread the cubes of spiced beef on to skewers, alternating with pepper and red onion. Grill for 8–10 minutes, turning once or twice, until cooked to your liking.

tip You can also use 2 x 125g (4¹/₂ oz) skinless chicken breast fillets in place of the rump steak. This will be 2 **POINTS** values per serving.

takes only
20
minutes

main meals

With these sensational dishes all ready in 30 minutes or less you'll be spoilt for choice whether you're looking for a satisfying meal for yourself or something for family or friends. There's Seared salmon with tangy avocado salsa, Moroccan braised cauliflower and couscous, and Cider pork hotpot, all a speedy and delicious solution to 'what's for dinner'.

page	recipe	✓	POINTS value
34	Sweet & sour Quorn		**2**
28	Pizza topped fish fillets		**2^1/$_2$**
48	Polenta pizza pie		**2^1/$_2$**
30	Thai red curry with prawns		**3**
42	Leek & butter bean crumble		**3**
45	Sweet potato stew		**3**
41	Sticky apricot chicken		**3^1/$_2$**
44	Honey & mustard pork		**3^1/$_2$**
29	Glazed salmon stir fry		**4**
33	Chinese meatballs		**4^1/$_2$**
35	Cheesy chicken goujons		**4^1/$_2$**
47	Cider pork hotpot		**5**
43	Cheesy ham & potato grill		**5^1/$_2$**
49	Spanish chicken & rice		**5^1/$_2$**
50	Peppered steak with balsamic onions		**6**
38	Beanie burgers with salsa	✓	**1^1/$_2$**
31	Turkey scallopine with lemon & caper sauce	✓	**2**
39	Moroccan braised cauliflower with couscous	✓	**2^1/$_2$**
40	Asian tuna parcels	✓	**2^1/$_2$**
37	Chickpea & pepper curry	✓	**2^1/$_2$**
23	Quick beef stroganoff	✓	**3**
52	Speedy turkey meatballs	✓	**3**
51	Provençal Quorn bake	✓	**3^1/$_2$**
27	Creamy leek & mushroom pasta	✓	**4**
36	Pan fried chicken with peas & bacon	✓	**4^1/$_2$**
24	Seared salmon with tangy avocado salsa	✓	**5^1/$_2$**
32	One pan beef & bean braise	✓	**5^1/$_2$**
25	Spiced lamb steaks with couscous	✓	**6**
46	Chicken & sweetcorn pie	✓	**6**
26	Stir fried pork & noodles	✓	**7**

A range of delicious recipes to choose from. Relax and enjoy. Index by *POINTS* values.

Serves 1

Takes 10 minutes

172 calories per serving

3 **POINTS** values per serving

3 **POINTS** values per recipe

low fat cooking spray

110 g (4 oz) lean beef stir fry or lean steak *cut into thin strips*

75 g (2³/₄ oz) chestnut mushrooms *sliced*

4 spring onions *sliced*

pinch ground paprika

75 ml (3 fl oz) beef stock *made using ¹/₄ stock cube*

2 tablespoons very low fat plain fromage frais

salt and freshly ground black pepper

Quick beef stroganoff

A satisfying, savoury supper dish that can be served on a bed of tagliatelle (60 g/2 oz dried weight) for an additional **POINTS** value of 3.

1 Heat a non stick frying pan on the hob and lightly coat with low fat cooking spray. Add the beef, followed by the mushrooms and spring onions. Stir fry for 3 minutes. Sprinkle in the paprika then pour in the beef stock.

2 Bubble rapidly for 30–60 seconds until the liquid is reduced and syrupy.

3 Remove the pan from the heat and leave for about 1 minute, then stir in the fromage frais and seasoning to taste.

Ⓨ **variation** *For a vegetarian version, replace the beef with a total of 250 g (9 oz) mixed mushrooms, and use vegetable stock instead of beef stock, for a **POINTS** value of ¹/₂.*

takes only **10** minutes

Serves 4

Takes 10 minutes

300 calories per serving

5¹/₂ **POINTS** values per serving

21¹/₂ **POINTS** values per recipe

4 x 125 g (4¹/₂ oz) skinless
   salmon fillets

low fat cooking spray

salt and freshly ground
   black pepper

for the salsa

1 medium avocado *peeled,
   stoned and diced*

100 g (3¹/₂ oz) cherry
   tomatoes *diced*

¹/₂ lime *grated zest and juice*

2 tablespoons coriander
   freshly chopped

Seared salmon with tangy avocado salsa

A quick, 'Summery' recipe that is just right served with 100 g (3¹/₂ oz) boiled new potatoes for an extra **POINTS** value of 1.

1 Preheat a non stick frying pan on the hob.

2 Lightly mist the salmon fillets with low fat cooking spray and season with salt and freshly ground black pepper. Cook for 2–3 minutes each side, or until cooked to your liking.

3 While the salmon is cooking, mix the salsa ingredients together and season. Serve the salsa spooned over the salmon.

tip *To prepare an avocado, cut in half then run a dessertspoon between the skin and the flesh to release it easily in one piece.*
Remove the stone and dice or slice as required.

takes only
10
minutes

Serves 2

Takes 12 minutes

288 calories per serving

6 *POINTS* values per serving

12 *POINTS* values per recipe

$^1/_2$ **lemon** *grated zest and juice*

1 red chilli *deseeded and diced*

1 teaspoon cumin seeds

salt and freshly ground black pepper

2 x 150 g (5$^1/_2$ oz) lean lamb steaks

low fat cooking spray

100 g (3$^1/_2$ oz) plain couscous

2 tablespoons coriander *freshly chopped*

Spiced lamb steaks with couscous

Cumin is a classic Middle Eastern spice that goes particularly well with lamb.

1 On a plate, mix together the lemon zest, half the chilli, cumin seeds and seasoning. Press the lamb steaks into the mixture to coat the meat.

2 Lightly coat a non stick frying pan with low fat cooking spray and fry the lamb steaks for 3–4 minutes each side, until done to your liking.

3 Meanwhile, mix the lemon juice and remaining chilli into the couscous in a bowl. Season and add 175 ml (6 fl oz) boiling water. Stir the mixture then cover the bowl and leave the couscous to stand for 5 minutes to soften.

4 Fluff up with a fork and mix in the coriander. Serve the lamb steaks on a bed of couscous.

takes only **12** minutes

Serves 1

Takes 12 minutes

350 calories per serving

7 **POINTS** values per serving

7 **POINTS** values per recipe

60 g (2 oz) medium egg
noodles

150 g (5¹/₂ oz) lean pork fillet
cut into 1 cm (¹/₂ inch) slices

¹/₂ teaspoon Chinese 5 spice
powder

low fat cooking spray

75 g (2³/₄ oz) button or
shiitake mushrooms *halved*

60 g (2 oz) broccoli *cut into
small florets*

1 tablespoon dark soy sauce

Stir fried pork & noodles

1 Cook the noodles in boiling water for 4 minutes, then drain and rinse in cold water. Meanwhile, toss the slices of pork with the Chinese 5 spice to coat.

2 Heat a non stick frying pan or wok on the hob, mist with low fat cooking spray, then cook each slice of pork for 1¹/₂ minutes on either side. Lift out to a plate and wipe the pan with kitchen paper.

3 Coat with a little more low fat cooking spray then stir fry the mushrooms and broccoli for 1–2 minutes. Add the soy sauce and 2 tablespoons water, reduce the heat, cover the pan and cook for 2 minutes until tender.

4 Add the noodles and pork to the frying pan or wok and stir fry for 1¹/₂ minutes until piping hot.
Serve immediately.

Ⓥ variation *For a vegetarian version, replace the pork fillet with 100 g (3¹/₂ oz) baby corn and increase the mushrooms to 110 g (4 oz). Stir fry the baby corn, broccoli and mushrooms, add the Chinese 5 spice powder with the soy sauce and water, and continue as above. This version will be a **POINTS** value of 3 per serving.*

takes only
12
minutes

Serves 1

Takes 12 minutes

301 calories per serving

4 *POINTS* values per serving

4 *POINTS* values per recipe

60 g (2 oz) penne
110 g (4 oz) leeks *sliced and rinsed*
low fat cooking spray
salt and freshly ground black pepper
110 g (4 oz) mushrooms *chopped roughly*
1 garlic clove *crushed*
1 teaspoon thyme *freshly chopped*
40 g (1¹/₂ oz) low fat soft cheese

Creamy leek & mushroom pasta

Low fat soft cheese makes a deliciously creamy sauce for pasta, with extra flavour added by garlic and thyme.

1 Tip the penne into a pan of boiling water and cook for 10–12 minutes until tender.

2 Meanwhile, coat the sliced leeks in low fat cooking spray in a non stick saucepan. Add seasoning and 2 tablespoons water, cover the pan and cook for 3 minutes

3 Add the mushrooms, garlic and thyme to the leeks, re-cover the pan and cook for 5 minutes. Stir the low fat soft cheese into the juices to make a creamy sauce.

4 Drain the pasta and toss together with the sauce. Serve in a warmed bowl.

takes only
12
minutes

Pizza topped fish fillets

Serves 4

Takes 5 minutes to prepare,

10 minutes to cook

156 calories per serving

2¹/₂ **POINTS** values per serving

10 **POINTS** values per recipe

4 x 125 g (4¹/₂ oz) pieces
   chunky haddock or cod loin

low fat cooking spray

salt and freshly ground
   black pepper

4 ripe tomatoes *sliced thickly*

12 stoned black olives *sliced*

2 tablespoons fresh basil
   shredded

60 g (2 oz) reduced fat
   mozzarella *diced*

This is a flavoursome way to bake fish fillets. Serve on a medium portion (60 g/2 oz dried weight) of tagliatelle for an extra **POINTS** value of 3.

1 Preheat the oven to Gas Mark 5/190ºC/fan oven 170ºC.

2 Place the pieces of fish on a baking tray that has been lightly greased with low fat cooking spray. Season the fish fillets and lay the tomato slices on top.

3 Scatter the olives, basil and mozzarella over and bake for 10 minutes until the cheese has melted and the fish flakes easily.

takes only **15** minutes

Serves 4

Takes 15 minutes

285 calories per serving

4 **POINTS** values per serving

17 **POINTS** values per recipe

2 tablespoons honey

5 tablespoons dark soy sauce

450 g (1 lb) skinless salmon
   fillet *cut into 2.5cm (1 inch)*
   chunks

low fat cooking spray

1 red pepper *deseeded and*
   sliced thinly

1 head Chinese leaf *shredded*
   roughly

1 tablespoon cornflour

Glazed salmon stir **fry**

① Stir the honey and 4 tablespoons of soy sauce together in a bowl, mix in the salmon and set aside.

② Heat a large non stick frying pan or wok on the hob and lightly coat with low fat cooking spray. Stir fry the pepper for 2 minutes then add the Chinese leaf and stir fry for 1 minute more. Pour in 1 tablespoon of soy sauce, cover the pan and cook for 2 minutes until tender. Tip into a warmed dish. Return the frying pan or wok to the heat.

③ Drain the salmon marinade into a jug, then stir-fry the cubed salmon for 2 minutes, stirring gently to colour evenly. Meanwhile, mix the cornflour into the marinade and add 100 ml ($3^1/_2$ fl oz) cold water. Pour this into the pan and simmer for $1^1/_2$ minutes until thickened.

serving suggestion *Serve the glazed salmon and stir-fried vegetables on a medium portion (150 g/$5^1/_2$oz) cooked rice for an additional* **POINTS** *value of 3.*

takes only
15
minutes

Serves 2

Takes 15 minutes

185 calories per serving

3 **POINTS** values per serving

6 **POINTS** values per recipe

225 g (8 oz) butternut
squash *peeled, deseeded
and diced*

100 g (3^1/$_2$ oz) green beans
trimmed and cut into thirds

low fat cooking spray

200 g (7 oz) raw peeled
tiger prawns

1 tablespoon Thai red curry
paste

100 ml (3^1/$_2$ fl oz) reduced
fat coconut milk

juice ^{1}/$_2$ lime

salt and freshly ground
black pepper

fresh coriander *to garnish*

Thai red curry with prawns

Add a scattering of freshly chopped coriander to this Thai curry for an authentic finishing touch.

❶ Add the diced butternut squash to a pan of boiling water. Cook for 4 minutes then add the green beans and cook for 4 minutes more. Drain the vegetables.

❷ Spray a non stick saucepan with low fat cooking spray then fry the prawns with the curry paste for 2 minutes. Pour in the coconut milk, then add the drained vegetables and simmer for 1 minute.

❸ Add the lime juice and seasoning to taste, just before serving. Garnish with fresh coriander.

takes only
15
minutes

Serves 2

Takes 15 minutes

137 calories per serving

2 **POINTS** values per serving

4 **POINTS** values per recipe

2 x 125 g (4¹/₂ oz) turkey
   breast steaks

¹/₂ **small lemon** grated zest
   and juice

**salt and freshly ground
   black pepper**

low fat cooking spray

1 garlic clove crushed

150 ml (5 fl oz) chicken stock

2 tablespoons parsley freshly
   chopped

1 tablespoon baby capers
   rinsed

Turkey scallopine with lemon & caper sauce

Mash 200 g (7 oz) of boiled potatoes with 2 tablespoons of skimmed milk to make a great accompaniment to soak up the sauce. Remember to add an extra **POINTS** value of 2¹/₂. Serve with broccoli for zero **POINTS** values.

❶ Place each turkey steak between two layers of cling film and flatten out to about 5mm (¹/₄ inch) thick, using a rolling pin or heavy based pan. Press the lemon zest and seasoning into the escalopes.

❷ Heat a non stick frying pan, lightly coat with low fat cooking spray then fry the turkey for 2¹/₂ minutes each side. Move to a plate and keep warm.

❸ Add the garlic to the pan and fry for a few seconds, without burning, then pour in the chicken stock and lemon juice and bubble fast for 3 minutes until the sauce has reduced by about half.

❹ Stir in the parsley and capers and pour the sauce over the turkey. Serve straightaway.

Serves 2

Takes 15 minutes

301 calories per serving

5¹/₂ **POINTS** values per serving

11 **POINTS** values per recipe

low fat cooking spray

225 g (8 oz) lean beef steak
  sliced thinly

2 rashers lean smoked back
  bacon *diced*

1 x 230 g can chopped
  tomatoes

150 ml (5 fl oz) beef stock
  made using $^1/_4$ *stock cube*

$^1/_2$ **teaspoon dried rosemary**

1 x 410 g can cannellini
  beans *drained and rinsed*

salt and freshly ground
  black pepper

One pan beef & bean braise

A rich savoury 'stew' that just needs some broccoli or green beans to accompany it for no extra **POINTS** values.

❶ Heat a non stick frying pan and lightly coat with low fat cooking spray. Brown the steak for 3 minutes over a high heat, then lift out to a plate.

❷ Add the bacon to the pan and stir fry for 1^1/$_2$ minutes. Tip in the tomatoes, stock, rosemary and beans.

❸ Return the steak to the pan, season and simmer for 8 minutes, uncovered. Serve in a deep plate, with spoons to scoop up the sauce.

takes only
15
minutes

Serves 4

Takes 20 minutes

188 calories per serving

4¹/₂ **POINTS** values per serving

18 **POINTS** values per recipe

❄

1 x 220 g can water chestnuts
  drained

500 g (1 lb 2 oz) extra lean
  pork mince

¹/₂ tablespoon Chinese 5
  spice powder

low fat cooking spray

2 tablespoons cornflour

3 tablespoons dark soy sauce

1 red chilli *deseeded and
  diced*

Chinese meatballs

Serve with a medium portion (150 g/5¹/₂ oz) of cooked white rice, adding a **POINTS** value of 3, and some zero **POINTS** value vegetables.

❶ Chop a third of the water chestnuts finely and mix these with the pork mince and Chinese 5 spice powder. Shape into 20 meatballs.

❷ Lightly coat a non stick frying pan with low fat cooking spray and cook the meatballs for 12–13 minutes over a medium heat, turning to brown them evenly.

❸ Meanwhile, mix the cornflour and soy sauce together in a measuring jug then add 300 ml (10 fl oz) cold water and the chilli.

❹ Slice the remaining water chestnuts in half and add these to the frying pan, along with the soy sauce mixture. Simmer for 2 minutes until the sauce is thickened and clear. Serve straightaway.

takes only
20
minutes

Serves 4

Takes 20 minutes

198 calories per serving

2 **POINTS** values per serving

8$^1/_2$ **POINTS** values per recipe

Ⓨ

2 tablespoons cornflour

4 tablespoons tomato
  ketchup

1 x 432 g can pineapple
  cubes in juice

low fat cooking spray

1 x 300 g pack frozen chicken
  style Quorn pieces

1 bunch spring onions *cut
  into chunky sections*

3 mixed peppers *deseeded
  and chopped roughly*

Sweet & sour Quorn

A quick and easy sweet and sour stir fry, using just a handful of ingredients. Serve with a medium portion (150 g/5$^1/_2$ oz) of cooked white rice, adding an extra **POINTS** value of 3.

❶   Blend the cornflour with 150 ml (5 fl oz) cold water in a jug, then whisk in the tomato ketchup and the juice from the canned pineapple.

❷   Heat a large non stick frying pan or wok on the hob, coat with low fat cooking spray and stir fry the Quorn pieces for 2 minutes. Add the spring onions and peppers and continue to cook, stirring, for 3–4 minutes. Pour in the sauce and simmer the mixture for 5 minutes, then stir in the cubes of pineapple and heat through for 2 minutes before serving.

variation   *Replace the Quorn with 300 g (10$^1/_2$ oz) diced skinless chicken breast for a **POINTS** value of 2$^1/_2$ per serving.*

takes only
20
minutes

Cheesy chicken goujons

Serves 4

Takes 20 minutes

239 calories per serving

4¹/₂ **POINTS** values per serving

17¹/₂ **POINTS** values per recipe

❄ before cooking, if using

fresh chicken

**4 x 125 g (4¹/₂ oz) skinless
   chicken breast fillets**
1 medium egg *beaten*
**salt and freshly ground
   black pepper**
2 medium slices bread
   (white or wholemeal)
**50 g (1³/₄ oz) finely grated
   Parmesan cheese**
low fat cooking spray

These extra tasty chicken goujons are great for sharing.

❶ Preheat the oven to Gas Mark 7/220°C/fan oven 200°C. Slice each chicken breast into seven or eight finger width strips. Beat the egg, with seasoning, in a shallow bowl.

❷ Whiz the bread to crumbs in a food processor and mix with the grated Parmesan on a large plate. Dip the chicken strips first in the egg then in the cheesy crumbs to coat.

❸ Place on a baking tray that has been lightly greased with low fat cooking spray, and mist the chicken goujons with a little more spray. Bake for 10–12 minutes until crisp, golden and cooked through.

takes only **20** *minutes*

Serves 2

Takes 20 minutes

221 calories per serving

4¹/₂ **POINTS** values per serving

9 **POINTS** values per recipe

salt and freshly ground
   black pepper
2 x 150 g (5¹/₂ oz) medium
   skinless chicken breasts
low fat cooking spray
2 rashers lean back bacon
   chopped
4 spring onions *chopped*
   roughly
¹/₄ chicken stock cube *made*
   up to 150 ml (5 fl oz)
100 g (3¹/₂ oz) frozen peas
1 Little Gem lettuce
   shredded roughly

Pan fried chicken with peas & bacon

Based on a French recipe for braised peas with lettuce, this dish is bursting with flavour. Serve with mashed potato (200 g/7 oz potato with 2 tablespoons of skimmed milk) for an additional **POINTS** value of 2¹/₂ .

1 Season the chicken breasts.

2 Mist a non stick frying pan with low fat cooking spray and brown the seasoned chicken breasts for 1 minute. Turn the chicken, add the bacon to the pan and fry for 1¹/₂ minutes.

3 Stir in the spring onions and cook for 30 seconds until bright green, then pour in the chicken stock and bring to a simmer. Cover the pan, reduce the heat and simmer for 10 minutes.

4 Stir in the frozen peas and lettuce, re-cover the pan and cook for 3–4 minutes until the peas are tender and the lettuce has wilted.

Serves 2

Takes 20 minutes

235 calories per serving

2$^1/_2$ **POINTS** values per serving

5 **POINTS** values per recipe

low fat cooking spray

1 red and 1 yellow pepper
deseeded and chopped
roughly

1 tablespoon medium curry
powder

1 x 230 g can chopped
tomatoes

100 g (3$^1/_2$ oz) low fat plain
yogurt

1 x 410 g can chickpeas
rinsed and drained

salt and freshly ground
black pepper

2 tablespoons coriander
freshly chopped (optional)

Chickpea & pepper curry

Serve this flavoursome curry with 150 g (5$^1/_2$ oz) cooked brown rice for an additional **POINTS** value of 3, or spoon it over a medium size 225 g (8 oz) jacket potato for an extra **POINTS** value of 2$^1/_2$.

❶ Spray a non stick saucepan with low fat cooking spray and fry the peppers for 4 minutes until slightly browned.

❷ Stir in the curry powder and cook for 30 seconds to develop the flavour, then mix in the chopped tomatoes, yogurt and chickpeas. Add seasoning, cover the pan and simmer for 10 minutes.

❸ Stir in the coriander, if using, just before serving.

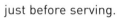
takes only **20** minutes

Serves 2

Takes 20 minutes

137 calories per serving

1¹/₂ **POINTS** values per serving

3¹/₂ **POINTS** values per recipe

❊ burgers only

**1 x 410 g can flageolet or
haricot beans** *rinsed and
drained*

1 medium egg white

**¹/₂ tablespoon medium
curry powder**

**salt and freshly ground
black pepper**

4 spring onions *chopped*

75 g (2³/₄ oz) carrot *peeled
and grated coarsely*

low fat cooking spray

2 tomatoes *diced small*

Beanie burgers with salsa

These curried bean and vegetable burgers are so easy to make and much tastier than ready-made versions.

1 Tip the beans into a food processor, adding the egg white, curry powder and seasoning. Pulse until mixed, but without processing to a smooth paste.

2 Stir in half the spring onions and all of the grated carrot and mix briefly.

3 Use damp hands to shape the sticky mixture into four burgers.

4 Lightly coat a non stick frying pan with low fat cooking spray and fry the burgers for 5 minutes each side over a medium heat.

5 While the burgers are cooking, mix the diced tomatoes with the rest of the spring onions and seasoning. Serve the salsa spooned over the hot burgers.

takes only
20
minutes

Serves 4

Takes 20 minutes

183 calories per serving

2$^1/_2$ **POINTS** values per serving

10$^1/_2$ **POINTS** values per recipe

❄ Ⓨ vegan

1 x 400 g can chopped
   tomatoes

1 tablespoon Moroccan
   spice blend

500 ml (18 fl oz) vegetable
   stock

1 medium cauliflower
   broken into florets
   (about 400 g/14 oz)

salt and freshly ground
   black pepper

200 g (7 oz) plain couscous

200 g (7 oz) fine green beans
   trimmed and halved

Moroccan braised cauliflower with couscous

Moroccan spice is a fragrant blend of spices such as cumin, coriander, chilli and lemon peel.

1 Place the chopped tomatoes, Moroccan spice and 150 ml (5 fl oz) of the stock in a large saucepan. Bring to a simmer, add the cauliflower and stir into the sauce with some seasoning. Cover and simmer for 10 minutes.

2 Pour the rest of the hot stock over the couscous in a bowl. Cover and leave to stand until softened, then fluff up with a fork.

3 Meanwhile, boil the green beans for 4 minutes, drain and rinse in cold water. Mix in with the cauliflower, re-cover the pan and simmer for 3 minutes until the vegetables are tender. Ladle over the couscous to serve.

variation *If you wish, add a 410 g can of drained chickpeas to the cauliflower for the last 3 minutes of cooking time. This will make the dish a* **POINTS** *value of 3$^1/_2$ per serving.*

takes only
20
minutes

Serves 4

Takes 20 minutes

200 calories per serving

2$\frac{1}{2}$ **POINTS** values per serving

9$\frac{1}{2}$ **POINTS** values per recipe

6 **spring onions** *sliced*

2 **garlic cloves** *peeled and sliced thinly*

5 cm (2 inch) **piece root ginger** *peeled and cut into matchsticks*

4 **heads pak choi**

4 x 150 g (5$\frac{1}{2}$ oz) fresh **tuna steaks**

4 **tablespoons dark soy sauce**

Asian tuna parcels

The aromatic flavourings of ginger, garlic and spring onions release a wonderful scent when the parcel is opened. Serve with 150 g (5$\frac{1}{2}$ oz) portion of cooked brown rice for an additional **POINTS** value of 3.

1 Preheat the oven to Gas Mark 6/200ºC/fan oven 180ºC.

2 Line a large roasting tin with a sheet of foil, big enough to double back over the roasting tin. Scatter half the spring onions, garlic and ginger over the base of the lined tin.

3 Cut each head of pak choi into quarters through the root then add to the roasting tin. Place the tuna steaks on top of the pak choi and scatter with the rest of the spring onions, garlic and ginger. Drizzle the soy sauce all over then crimp the edges of the foil tightly to make a large parcel.

4 Bake in the oven for 12 minutes, then carefully undo the foil and serve the tuna on the bed of pak choi.

takes only **20** minutes

Serves 2

Takes 25 minutes

253 calories per serving

3$\frac{1}{2}$ **POINTS** values per serving

7 **POINTS** values per recipe

2 x 150 g (5$\frac{1}{2}$ oz) skinless
chicken breast fillets

2 tablespoons apricot jam

1 tablespoon tomato ketchup

1 tablespoon lemon juice

1 teaspoon smooth mustard
e.g. Dijon or English

salt

pinch cayenne pepper or
chilli powder

Sticky apricot chicken

Apricot jam gives the barbecue style sauce sweetness, then there's a gentle kick from the mustard and cayenne pepper. Serve with broccoli and 150 g (5$\frac{1}{2}$ oz) new potatoes for an additional **POINTS** value of 1$\frac{1}{2}$.

1 Preheat the oven to Gas Mark 7/220ºC/fan oven 200ºC. Line a roasting tin with foil or baking parchment to stop the glaze sticking to the tin.

2 Lightly slash the chicken on both sides and place in the roasting tin.

3 Mix the jam with the ketchup, lemon juice and mustard then season with salt and a pinch of cayenne pepper or chilli powder. Brush half the glaze over the chicken and roast for 10 minutes.

4 Turn the chicken over and brush with the other half of the glaze. Cook for a further 10 minutes until cooked through and deliciously sticky.

takes only
25
minutes

Serves 2

Takes 25 minutes

250 calories per serving

3 **POINTS** values per serving

6$^1/_2$ **POINTS** values per recipe

Ⓥ

low fat cooking spray

250 g (9 oz) leeks *trimmed,*
rinsed and sliced

salt and freshly ground
black pepper

150 ml (5 fl oz) vegetable
stock

1 medium slice bread *(white*
or wholemeal)

40 g (1$^1/_2$ oz) half fat
mature cheese *grated*

1 x 410 g can butter beans
rinsed and drained

2 teaspoons grain mustard

Leek & butter bean crumble

This rustic dish with a cheesy crust is perfect served with steamed broccoli florets.

❶ Preheat the oven to Gas Mark 5/190ºC/fan oven 170ºC.

❷ Lightly coat a non stick saucepan with low fat cooking spray, add the leeks and seasoning and toss to coat. Add 3 tablespoons of the stock, cover the pan and cook for 4 minutes until tender.

❸ In the meantime, roughly tear up the bread and whiz to crumbs in a food processor, or use a hand held blender. Mix with the grated cheese.

❹ Add the drained butter beans, mustard and remaining stock to the leeks, season and stir to mix then tip into a baking dish. Cover with the cheesy crumbs and mist with low fat cooking spray. Bake for 15 minutes until crisp, golden and bubbling.

takes only
25
minutes

Cheesy ham & potato grill

Serves 4

Takes 25 minutes

283 calories per serving

5½ *POINTS* values per serving

22½ *POINTS* values per recipe

750 g (1 lb 10 oz) new
   potatoes *sliced to a
   thickness of 3–4 mm*

½ vegetable or chicken
   stock cube

150 g (5½ oz) frozen peas

75 g (2¾ oz) low fat soft
   cheese

salt and freshly ground
   black pepper

100 g (3½ oz) wafer thin
   smoked ham *chopped*

100 g (3½ oz) Brie *sliced*

A delicious dish with ham and melted Brie, this is very satisfying, easy and family friendly.

1 Preheat the grill. Add the sliced potatoes and stock cube to a large pan of boiling water. Cover and bring back to the boil, then simmer for 6 minutes.

2 Add the peas and cook for 2 minutes, or until tender.

3 Blend the soft cheese with 3 tablespoons of the cooking water, plus seasoning, to make a sauce.

4 Drain the potatoes and peas and layer into a dish with the ham. Drizzle on the sauce and top with the sliced Brie. Grill for 3–5 minutes until the cheese starts to melt.

takes only
25
minutes

450 g (1 lb) **swede** *peeled and diced*

450 g (1 lb) **carrots** *peeled and diced*

salt and freshly ground black pepper

low fat cooking spray

4 x 150 g (5¹/₂ oz) lean pork steaks

2 tablespoons honey

2 tablespoons grain mustard

juice ¹/₂ lemon

Honey & mustard pork

These pork steaks, in a delicious sweet-sharp sauce, need nothing more than some green cabbage to go with them for no additional **POINTS** values.

1 Add the diced swede and carrots to a large pan of boiling water. Cover and simmer for 15–20 minutes until tender. Drain well, mash roughly and season to taste.

2 When the vegetables have been cooking for about 10 minutes, heat a large non stick frying pan on the hob and mist with low fat cooking spray. Season the pork steaks and brown for 3–4 minutes on each side, depending on their thickness, or until cooked through.

3 Mix the honey, mustard and lemon juice together and pour over the pork steaks. Cook for 1 minute more, turning the pork steaks to glaze them in the sauce. Serve with the mashed carrot and swede.

takes only **25** minutes

Serves 4

Takes 25 minutes

245 calories per serving

3 **POINTS** values per serving

11^1/$_2$ **POINTS** values per recipe

 vegan

low fat cooking spray

1 large onion *chopped*
roughly

3 mixed peppers *deseeded*
and chopped roughly

2 tablespoons medium
curry powder

500 g (1 lb 2 oz) sweet
potatoes *peeled and diced*

60 g (2 oz) reduced fat
peanut butter

salt and freshly ground
black pepper

2 tablespoons coriander
freshly chopped

Sweet potato stew

Based on an African recipe, this mildly curried hearty vegetable stew is thickened and flavoured with reduced fat peanut butter, which gives the sauce a rich, velvety texture.

1 Lightly coat a flameproof casserole with low fat cooking spray, add the onion and peppers and stir fry for 5 minutes until browned.

2 Stir in the curry powder and sweet potatoes and toss to coat everything in the spices.

3 Add 400 ml (14 fl oz) boiling water then stir in the peanut butter. Bring to a simmer, season, cover and cook for 12 minutes until tender. Stir in the coriander just before serving and ladle the stew into warm bowls.

takes only
25
minutes

Serves 1

Takes 25 minutes

425 calories per serving

6 **POINTS** values per serving

6 **POINTS** values per recipe

❄ before grilling

200 g (7 oz) potatoes *peeled
    and diced*

$^1/_2$ chicken stock cube

salt and freshly ground
    black pepper

1 x 125 g (4$^1/_2$ oz) skinless
    chicken breast fillet *diced*

low fat cooking spray

150 g (5$^1/_2$ oz) leeks *sliced*

60 g (2 oz) frozen sweetcorn

40 g (1$^1/_2$ oz) low fat soft
    cheese

Chicken & sweetcorn pie

This is ideal comfort food for one, but the recipe can easily be multiplied to make a family size pie.

❶ Add the potatoes and stock cube to a pan of boiling water, cover and cook for 10–12 minutes until tender. Drain, reserving the stock, and mash the potatoes with 2 tablespoons of the stock and seasoning.

❷ Meanwhile, stir fry the chicken in low fat cooking spray in a non stick saucepan for 3 minutes until browned. Stir in the leeks, 4 tablespoons of stock and seasoning.

❸ Cover the pan and cook for 5 minutes. Add the sweetcorn and cook for 2 minutes more. Preheat the grill to high.

❹ Stir the soft cheese into the chicken mixture to make a sauce, check the seasoning then tip into a small baking dish. Spread the mashed potato on top, mist with low fat cooking spray and grill for 5 minutes to brown the top.

takes only
25
minutes

46 main meals

Serves 4

Takes 30 minutes

273 calories per serving

5 **POINTS** values per serving

20 **POINTS** values per recipe

350 g (12 oz) small new
potatoes *quartered*

**salt and freshly ground
black pepper**

450 g (1 lb) extra lean pork
fillet *diced*

low fat cooking spray

1 eating apple *cored and
cut into wedges*

300 g (10¹⁄₂ oz) leeks
trimmed, rinsed and sliced

300 ml (10 fl oz) dry cider

2 tablespoons cornflour

Cider pork hotpot

Pork and apples are a fabulous combination, enhanced here by the addition of cider for extra flavour. Serve with carrots and lightly cooked green cabbage for no extra **POINTS** values.

❶ Add the potatoes to a pan of boiling water and simmer for 5–6 minutes.

❷ Meanwhile, season the diced pork. Spray a flameproof casserole dish with low fat cooking spray and brown the pork for 3 minutes. Add the apple wedges and fry for one more minute.

❸ Stir in the leeks and drained potatoes, then pour in the cider and 150 ml (5 fl oz) boiling water. Season well, bring to the boil and simmer, covered, for 18 minutes.

❹ Blend the cornflour with a little cold water, then stir it into the casserole and simmer for 1–2 minutes until thickened.

tip *For a one pot dish, add the raw potatoes with the leeks. Cook the hotpot for 5–10 minutes longer, until the potatoes are tender.*

takes only
30
minutes

Serves 4

Takes 30 minutes

146 calories per serving

2¹/₂ **POINTS** values per serving

10¹/₂ **POINTS** values per recipe

Ⓥ

75 g (2 ³/₄ oz) instant polenta
or cornmeal

25 g (1 oz) freshly grated
Parmesan cheese

salt and freshly ground
black pepper

low fat cooking spray

175 g (6 oz) cherry tomatoes
halved

110 g (4 oz) mushrooms *sliced*

1 yellow pepper *deseeded*
and sliced thinly

60 g (2 oz) reduced fat
mozzarella *diced*

Polenta pizza pie

Polenta makes a good low **POINTS** value alternative to a dough base.

❶ Preheat the oven to Gas Mark 6/200ºC/fan oven 180ºC.

❷ Bring 400 ml (14 fl oz) water to the boil in a large non stick saucepan. Tip in the polenta in a steady stream and stir until bubbling.

❸ Reduce the heat and cook for 5 minutes, stirring occasionally, until well thickened. Remove from the heat and stir in 15 g (¹/₂ oz) Parmesan cheese, salt and freshly ground black pepper.

❹ Pour the warm polenta into to a 23 cm (9 inch) tart tin that has been lightly greased with low fat cooking spray. Alternatively, simply spread out to a circle on a greased baking tray.

❺ Toss the vegetables in a bowl, with seasoning, and low fat cooking spray then pile them on to the polenta base.

Cook on a high shelf in the oven for 10 minutes, then scatter the mozzarella and remaining Parmesan on top and cook for another 5 minutes until melted.

takes only
30
minutes

Serves 4

Takes 30 minutes

401 calories per serving

5$^1/_2$ **POINTS** values per serving

21$^1/_2$ **POINTS** values per recipe

450 g (1 lb) skinless chicken
   breast fillet *diced*

low fat cooking spray

salt and freshly ground
   black pepper

1 onion *chopped finely*

2 red peppers *deseeded and
   diced*

1.2 litres (2 pints) hot
   chicken stock

250 g (9 oz) paella or risotto
   rice

150 g (5$^1/_2$ oz) frozen peas

Spanish chicken & rice

1 In a casserole or large saucepan, brown the chicken in low fat cooking spray for 3 minutes. Season and transfer to a plate.

2 Add the onion to the casserole and stir fry for 2 minutes. Mix in the peppers and 4 tablespoons of stock. Cover and cook for 3–4 minutes until until the onion and peppers are tender.

3 Stir the rice into the juices, return the chicken to the pan and add 850 ml (1$^1/_2$ pints) of the stock. Simmer, uncovered, for 18 minutes until tender, stirring occasionally.

4 Add extra stock as needed if the rice looks too dry (the finished dish should have a slightly soupy consistency). Stir in the frozen peas for the last couple of minutes of cooking. Serve ladled into bowls.

ⓨ **variation** *You can add a couple of diced courgettes along with the peppers, to replace the chicken, and use vegetable stock. This will be a **POINTS** value of 3$^1/_2$ per serving.*

takes only **30** minutes

Serves 2

Takes 30 minutes

421 calories per serving

6 **POINTS** values per serving

12¹/₂ **POINTS** values per recipe

500 g (1 lb 2 oz) potatoes
    peeled and diced

¹/₂ beef stock cube

low fat cooking spray

1 large onion *sliced thinly*

2 tablespoons balsamic
    vinegar

1 tablespoon redcurrant jelly

salt and coarsely ground
    black pepper

2 x 110 g (4 oz) fillet or
    medallion steaks

Peppered steak with balsamic onions

Try this mouth-watering recipe for a special occasion.

❶ Preheat the oven to Gas Mark 7/220°C/fan oven 200°C. Add the potatoes and beef stock cube to a pan of boiling water. Cook for 4 minutes then drain (reserving the stock), and tip on to a baking tray.

❷ Lightly coat with low fat cooking spray, spread out and cook in the oven for 20–25 minutes until crisp and golden.

❸ Meanwhile, fry the onion in low fat cooking spray for 5 minutes over a high heat, until browned. Add the balsamic vinegar and 6 tablespoons of the reserved stock. Cover the pan and cook for 20 minutes until tender. Stir in the redcurrant jelly until melted.

❹ Season the steaks generously with coarsely ground pepper and a little salt. Fry for 3–4 minutes on each side, in a non stick frying pan, or until done to your liking. Serve with roasted potatoes and sticky onions.

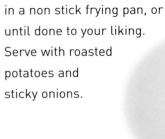

Serves 4

Takes 30 minutes

276 calories per serving

3½ **POINTS** values per serving

14 **POINTS** values per recipe

800 g (1 lb 11 oz) potatoes
cut into 2 cm (³/₄ inch) dice

1 vegetable stock cube

low fat cooking spray

8 x 51 g frozen Quorn pieces

2 garlic cloves *crushed*

1 x 400 g can chopped
tomatoes

1 heaped teaspoon dried
Herbes de Provence or
mixed herbs

salt and freshly ground
black pepper

Provençal Quorn bake

1 Preheat the oven to Gas Mark 7/220°C/fan oven 200°C.

2 Add the potatoes and stock cube to a pan of boiling water. Bring back to the boil, cover and simmer for 4 minutes. Drain, reserving 200 ml (7 fl oz) of the cooking water, then shake up the potatoes lightly to roughen the edges (this helps to crisp them up).

3 Meanwhile, spray a non stick frying pan with a little low fat cooking spray and brown the Quorn pieces for 1½ minutes. Transfer to a baking dish.

4 Add the garlic to the frying pan and cook for 20–30 seconds, without burning, then tip in the tomatoes, add the herbs and reserved cooking water. Season, bring to a simmer and pour over the Quorn pieces in the dish.

5 Scatter the potatoes on top of the pieces and sauce then lightly coat them with low fat cooking spray.

Bake in the oven for 18 minutes until the potatoes are crisp on top.

takes only **30** minutes

Serves 4

Takes 30 minutes

208 calories per serving

3 **POINTS** values per serving

12 **POINTS** values per recipe

❄

1 onion

low fat cooking spray

200 g (7 oz) mushrooms
chopped roughly

salt and freshly ground
black pepper

300 ml (10 fl oz) chicken stock

2 wholewheat crispbreads
crushed

500 g (1 lb 2 oz) turkey mince

1 x 400 g can chopped
tomatoes

Speedy turkey meatballs

Serve on a bed of tagliatelle (60 g/2 oz dried weight for an extra **POINTS** value of 3) that has been mixed with some lightly cooked green vegetables such as broccoli and green beans.

1 Chop half the onion and fry in low fat cooking spray in a casserole for 2 minutes. Stir in the mushrooms, seasoning and 3 tablespoons of stock, cover the pan and cook for 2 minutes.

2 Meanwhile, grate the second half of the onion into a bowl, add the rye crispbread crumbs and moisten with 2 tablespoons of stock. Mix in the turkey mince and seasoning and shape into 20 meatballs.

3 Add the tomatoes and the rest of the stock to the onion and mushroom mixture. Season and simmer the sauce for about 5 minutes.

4 Meanwhile, brown the meatballs in low fat cooking spray in a non stick frying pan for 5 minutes, turning to colour evenly. Add them to the sauce and simmer, uncovered, for 15 minutes, until cooked through.

tip *If you don't have a rolling pin to crush the crispbread on your chopping board, use a filled can.*

takes only 30 minutes

sweet things

Why not make a batch of Apple pancakes or Strawberry shortcakes and share with friends. Or, when only chocolate will do, try the indulgent Chocolate fondue served with delicious fruits. Enjoy this range of delicious desserts.

For everyone who loves desserts. Index by *POINTS* values.

Serves 2

Takes 5 minutes

119 calories per serving

2¹/₂ **POINTS** values per serving

4¹/₂ **POINTS** values per recipe

1 large ripe mango

1 x 150 g pot 0% fat Greek
    yogurt

2 passionfruit

Mango & passionfruit fool

A ripe mango should feel just soft to the touch, and smell perfumed, while a ripe passionfruit should have a slightly dimpled skin, but feel fairly heavy, indicating that it is still full of juice.

❶ Peel the mango using a vegetable peeler, then chop the flesh away from the central stone. Blend to a purée in a food processor, or using a hand held blender.

❷ Mix in the yogurt until smooth then stir in the seeds and juice of one passionfruit. Divide between two glasses.

❸ Spoon the seeds and juice of the second passionfruit on top of the fools before serving.

tip *You can eat the fool straightaway or it can be prepared in advance and chilled for up to 2 hours.*

Serves 4

Takes 6 minutes to prepare

95 calories per serving

1½ **POINTS** values per serving

5½ **POINTS** values per recipe

Ⓥ

200 g (7 oz) very low fat
   plain fromage frais
250 g (9 oz) Quark
grated zest ½ lime
1½ tablespoons
   granulated sweetener
1 x 411 g peach halves in
   juice *drained*

Peach flip

This lusciously creamy dessert is livened up with a hint of fresh lime zest.
The recipe also works well with tinned apricots in juice, for the same
POINTS value per serving.

❶ Whisk the fromage frais and Quark together until smooth, stirring in the
lime zest and sweetener to flavour the mixture.

❷ Thinly slice two of the peach halves to use for garnish, then chop the
rest of the peaches into small cubes.

❸ Stir the diced peaches into the fromage frais
mixture and divide between four dessert glasses.
Top with the sliced peaches to serve.

takes only
6
minutes

Serves 2

Takes 7 minutes

109 calories per serving

1¹/₂ **POINTS** values per serving

3¹/₂ **POINTS** values per recipe

Ⓥ

1 x 411 g can pear quarters
   in juice *drained*

freshly grated nutmeg

1 x 210 g can apricots in
   juice

4 tablespoons very low fat
   plain fromage frais

Spicy pears with apricot sauce

A little spice lifts the flavour of this fast fruity pud, but if you don't have any nutmeg in the cupboard, you can use a little mixed spice or cinnamon instead.

❶ Preheat a non stick frying pan on the hob, and pat the pear quarters dry on kitchen paper. Add the pears to the pan and fry for 2 minutes either side until caramelised. Grate a little nutmeg over the pears as they cook.

❷ Meanwhile, tip the apricots and their juice into a liquidiser and blend until smooth, or use a hand held blender. Pour into two bowls, add the pan fried pears and top with the fromage frais and an extra grating of nutmeg.

takes only
7
minutes

Serves 4

Takes 10 minutes

138 calories per serving

2 *POINTS* values per serving

8¹/₂ *POINTS* values per recipe

Ⓥ

10 sponge fingers

¹/₂ **lemon** *grated zest and juice*

100 g (3¹/₂ oz) low fat soft cheese

1 x 135 g pot low fat custard

100 g (3¹/₂ oz) blueberries *reserving 10 for the top*

1 tsp caster sugar *for dusting*

Lemon & blueberry charlottes

A deliciously creamy dessert that's perfect for serving to friends as it looks so special.

❶ Cut each sponge finger lengthways and then in half to make four short pieces. Mix 1 tablespoon of lemon juice with 1 tablespoon of water and brush this all over the sponge fingers. Arrange ten pieces of sponge finger upright around the sides of four ramekins.

❷ Whisk the rest of the lemon juice and the zest into the soft cheese and custard, then fold in all but 10 of the blueberries. Spoon into the ramekins, inside the lining of sponge fingers.

❸ Garnish with the reserved blueberries, a little extra lemon zest and a sprinkling of caster sugar if you like.

serving suggestion *Serve straightaway, or cover and chill until ready to serve.*

takes only
10
minutes

Cherry brûlée

Serves 2

Takes 10 minutes

175 calories per serving

3 **POINTS** values per serving

5¹/₂ **POINTS** values per recipe

Ⓥ

150 g (5¹/₂ oz) cherries

125 g (4¹/₂ oz) Quark

100 g (3¹/₂ oz) very low fat
   plain fromage frais

¹/₂ teaspoon vanilla extract

50 g (1³/₄ oz) Demerara
   sugar

Quark is a very low fat soft cheese that is ideal for making desserts.

❶ Preheat the grill to its highest setting.

❷ Stone the cherries and place in the base of two ramekins. Whisk the Quark and fromage frais together with the vanilla extract until smooth. Spoon on top of the fruit and level the surface.

❸ Sprinkle the Demerara sugar evenly over the top and mist lightly with water (this helps the sugar to dissolve quickly under the grill). Pop under the hot grill and cook for 2–3 minutes until the sugar has melted and begun to caramelise.

❹ Allow the brûlées to cool, and the caramel to harden, for a couple of minutes before eating.

tip *You can use an olive stoner to stone cherries if you have one, but if not, place the cherries on a chopping board and lightly crush with a rolling pin or filled can to release the stones.*

takes only
10
minutes

Serves 4

Takes 10 minutes

207 calories per serving

4 **POINTS** values per serving

15¹/₂ **POINTS** values per recipe

Ⓥ

25 g (1 oz) cocoa powder

1 x 170 g can evaporated milk

25 g (1 oz) milk chocolate
  chopped

2 medium bananas *peeled*
  and sliced

3 clementines or satsumas
  peeled and segmented

200 g (7 oz) strawberries

Chocolate fondue

This clever chocolate fondue sauce is rich and indulgent, but surprisingly low in **POINTS** value.

❶ Place the cocoa in a non stick saucepan and gradually stir in the evaporated milk to make a smooth sauce.

❷ Add the chocolate and place the pan over a medium heat. Bring to a simmer, stirring, then cook for 1 minute until thickened.

❸ Pour into small individual bowls and serve with the fruit, to dip into the chocolate fondue sauce.

takes only
10
minutes

Serves 1

Takes 10 minutes

188 calories per serving

2¹/₂ **POINTS** values per serving

2¹/₂ **POINTS** values per recipe

1 medium orange *peeled and sliced*

1 medium banana *peeled and sliced thickly*

1 passionfruit

1 tablespoon very low fat plain fromage frais

Baked banana with passionfruit

Passionfruit adds a wonderful, exotic fragrance to these easy fruit parcels.

❶ Preheat the oven to Gas Mark 6/200ºC/fan oven 180ºC.

❷ Place a large square of foil on a baking tray. Sit the orange slices in the centre, add the banana then scoop the seeds from the passionfruit and place on the banana.

❸ Seal the parcel tightly, crimping and sealing the foil so that the juices can't escape. Bake for 7 minutes, then open up carefully and serve topped with the fromage frais.

Serves 4

Takes 15 minutes

185 calories per serving

2¹/₂ **POINTS** values per serving

10 **POINTS** values per recipe

❄ pancakes only Ⓥ

2 tablespoons caster sugar

1 teaspoon ground cinnamon

110 g (4 oz) self-raising flour

pinch of salt

1 medium egg

125 ml (4 fl oz) skimmed milk

2 eating apples

low fat cooking spray

Apple pancakes

These little pancake stacks are delicious served with 1 tablespoon of very low fat plain fromage frais or 0% fat Greek yogurt, for an extra **POINTS** value of ¹/₂ per serving.

❶ Mix the sugar and cinnamon together, reserving 2 teaspoons for sprinkling at the end, then place the remainder in a mixing bowl.

❷ Sift in the flour and a pinch of salt. Make a well in the centre then break in the egg. Gradually whisk in the milk to give a smooth batter. Peel one of the apples and coarsely grate it into the batter, discarding the core.

❸ Lightly coat a non stick frying pan with low fat cooking spray then drop in 4 separate tablespoons of batter. Cook for 1¹/₂ minutes until browned underneath and bubbly on top, then flip over and cook for 1 minute on the other side. Keep warm and repeat to make a total of 12 pancakes. Core and thinly slice the remaining apple.

❹ To serve, layer three pancakes per serving with a quarter of the sliced apple, sprinkling with the cinnamon sugar as you go.

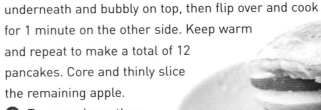

takes only 15 minutes

Serves 4

Takes 15 minutes

41 calories per serving

$^1/_2$ **POINTS** values per serving

$1^1/_2$ **POINTS** values per recipe

250 g (9 oz) frozen
raspberries *defrosted*

1 orange *juice + 1$^1/_2$
teaspoon grated zest*

**3 tablespoons granulated
sweetener**

2 medium egg white

Poached meringues with raspberry coulis

❶ Process the raspberries to a purée with the orange juice, using a food processor or a hand held blender. Press through a sieve to remove the seeds then stir in 1 tablespoon of the sweetener. Divide between four shallow bowls.

❷ Bring a frying pan of water to the boil. Using a food processor or hand held blender, whisk the egg whites until stiff then beat in 2 tablespoons of sweetener and 1 teaspoon of the orange zest.

❸ Dip an ice cream scoop into a jug of cold water, then take a scoop of meringue and put into the boiling water using another spoon to push the meringue into the water. Repeat to make four meringues from half the mixture. Poach for 1 minute each side.

❹ With a draining spoon, lift the meringues out of the water and place a meringue in each bowl. Repeat with the remaining mixture to make four more meringues. Serve immediately, garnished with the rest of the orange zest.

takes only **15** minutes

Takes 20 minutes

254 calories per serving

3¹/₂ **POINTS** values per serving

7¹/₂ **POINTS** values per recipe

75 g (2³/₄ oz) risotto rice
  e.g. arborio

300 ml (10 fl oz) skimmed
  milk

³/₄ teaspoon ground cinnamon

60 g (2 oz) dried apricots
  diced

1 tablespoon caster sugar

Fruity cinnamon rice pudding

A quick hob-cooked version of rice pudding, flavoured with sweet cinnamon.

❶ Place the rice in a non stick saucepan with the milk, cinnamon and 100 ml (3¹/₂ fl oz) water. Bring to the boil, stirring occasionally so that the rice doesn't stick to the base of the pan, especially towards the end of the cooking time.

❷ Simmer for about 18 minutes until most of the liquid has been absorbed and the rice is tender. It should have a soft, slightly soupy consistency when ready.

❸ Just before serving stir in the apricots and sugar.

2 x 45 g large sheets frozen
   filo pastry *defrosted*
25 g (1 oz) low fat
   polyunsaturated
   margarine *melted*
2 ripe pears *halved*
2 teaspoons caster sugar
100 g (3¹/₂ oz) raspberries

Fruity filo tarts

Try to use ripe pears for these fruity tarts, so that the juices can run and start to caramelise as they cook.

1 Preheat the oven to Gas Mark 6/200°C/fan oven 180°C.

2 Brush each sheet of filo lightly with the melted margarine. Fold in half lengthways, then into thirds, and cut each folded sheet into two rectangles.

3 Place on a baking tray and brush the top with melted margarine. Remove the cores from the pears using a teaspoon then slice and arrange on the pastry bases. Sprinkle with sugar and bake on a high shelf for 8 minutes.

4 Scatter the raspberries on top and cook for a further 4 minutes. Serve warm.

tip *You can find frozen filo pastry packs that weigh 270 g for 6 sheets in major supermarkets. This will give you the size of sheet you need for this recipe.*

takes only
20
minutes

Serves 4

Takes 25 minutes

240 calories per serving

4¹/₂ **POINTS** values per serving

17 **POINTS** values per recipe

❈ without the sauce Ⓨ

low fat cooking spray

60 g (2 oz) low fat
   polyunsaturated
   margarine

60 g (2 oz) caster sugar

1 medium egg

100 g (3¹/₂ oz) self raising
   flour

1 small lemon *grated zest,
   plus 2 tablespoons juice*

4 heaped teaspoons lemon
   curd

Lemon curd sponges

These light sponge puddings have a luscious and delightfully tart lemon curd sauce poured over them.

❶ Preheat the oven to Gas Mark 4/180°C/fan oven 160°C. Lightly grease four mini pudding basins with low fat cooking spray and place them on a baking tray.

❷ Using an electric whisk, beat together the margarine, sugar, egg, flour, lemon zest and 1 tablespoon of lemon juice, for 2 minutes. Spoon into the pudding basins to come about half way up, then bake on the centre shelf for 15 minutes.

❸ Meanwhile, stir together the lemon curd, 1 tablespoon of lemon juice and 1 tablespoon of water in a small saucepan and heat gently to make the sauce.

❹ Turn the puddings out of the moulds and serve warm with the sauce spooned over.

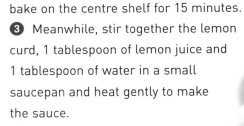

takes only
25
minutes

Strawberry shortcakes

Serves 6

Takes 25 minutes

203 calories per serving

3 **POINTS** values per serving

18$\frac{1}{2}$ **POINTS** values per recipe

❄ unfilled shortcakes only

225 g (8 oz) self-raising flour

pinch of salt

25 g (1 oz) low fat
polyunsaturated
margarine

25 g (1 oz) caster sugar

300 g (10$\frac{1}{2}$ oz) very low fat
plain fromage frais

6 heaped teaspoons low
sugar strawberry jam

110 g (4 oz) strawberries
sliced

An American style dessert of freshly baked sweet scones with a creamy filling and fresh berries.

❶ Preheat the oven to Gas Mark 7/220°C/fan oven 200°C.

❷ Reserve 2 teaspoons of flour for rolling out, then sift the rest into a mixing bowl with a pinch of salt. Rub in the margarine until the mixture looks like breadcrumbs then stir in all but 1 teaspoon of the sugar (keep this for the tops).

❸ Mix in 200 g (7 oz) of the fromage frais, with a knife, to make a soft but not sticky dough. Add a little water if needed.

❹ Pat the dough out on a floured work surface, to a depth of 2 cm (³/₄ inch), then use a floured 6 cm (2$\frac{1}{2}$ inch) cutter to stamp out six rounds. Transfer to a baking tray, brush the tops of the shortcakes with water and sprinkle with the reserved sugar. Bake for 10–12 minutes until risen and golden.

❺ Meanwhile, stir the strawberry jam into the remaining fromage frais. Cool the shortcakes for a few minutes then split and top with the fromage frais mixture and strawberries.

Serves 6

Takes 25 minutes to cook and

assemble

144 calories per serving

2 **POINTS** values per serving

11 **POINTS** values per recipe

low fat cooking spray

5 medium egg whites

50 g (1³/₄ oz) plain flour

pinch of salt

110 g (4 oz) caster sugar

1 x 410 g can peach slices in
   juice drained and chopped

zest of ¹/₂ lime

1 x 150 g pot 0% fat Greek
   yogurt

Peach angel roulade

❶ Preheat the oven to Gas Mark 4/180°C/fan oven 160°C. Line a 20 x 30cm (8 x 12 inch) Swiss roll tin with baking parchment and lightly mist with low fat cooking spray.

❷ Whisk the egg whites to stiff peaks in a large bowl. Sift in the flour, a pinch of salt and all but 2 teaspoons of the sugar and fold together. Spread out in the tin and bake on the centre shelf of the oven for 12–15 minutes until set, golden and beginning to pull away from the edges of the tin.

❸ Lay another sheet of baking parchment on the work surface and sprinkle with the reserved sugar. Turn out the angel sponge cake on to the paper. Peel off the lining paper and roll up the roulade from one long side, wrapping the sugared paper inside as you go.

❹ Leave to cool. Mix the peaches with the lime zest and set aside.

❺ To serve, unroll the roulade, spread with the yogurt then scatter the peaches over. Roll up and cut into slices.

takes only
25
minutes